Theory Paper   Grade 7   2014   A
Model Answers

1 *There are many ways of completing this question. The specimen completion* ~~below would receive full marks.~~   (15)
The passage is adapted from C. P. E. Bach, 'Suscepit Israel' from Magnificat, H. 772, beginning at bar 9.

2 *There are many ways of completing this question. The specimen completion below would receive full marks.*   (15)
The passage is adapted from J. S. Bach, Chorale 'Wo Gott zum Haus nicht gibt', BWV 438 (Riemenschneider No. 157).

3 *There are many ways of completing this question. Either of the specimen completions below would receive full marks.* (20)

EITHER

(a) *The source of the passage is Mendelssohn, Frühlingsglaube, Op. 9 No. 8, beginning in bar 6.*

OR

(b) *The given opening is printed in grey in order to distinguish it from the completion, but candidates must include the opening in their answer.*

trumpet

4   *The source of the extract is Schubert, Scherzo in D flat from Two Scherzos, D. 593.*

(a)    (3)

(b)   Bar 25   V⁷a / V⁷a major

Bar 28   IVc / IVc major   } Key   E major   (7)

(c)   *All possible answers are shown on the extract reproduced below.*

B   Bar   21   (2)
C   Bar   24   (2)
D   Bars   15–16   (2)
E   Bar   17   (2)

(d)   (i)   true   (2)
(ii)   false   (2)
(iii)   true   (2)

(e)   Schubert   (1)

5   *The source of the extract is Finzi, second movement of Cello Concerto, Op. 40, beginning at bar 78.*

   (a)   sonorous / resonant / rich / rich tone   (2)
         unison / all players / no longer divided / everyone playing the same notes   (2)

   (b)   (i)   Clarinets   (3)

         (ii)   Horns   (3)

   (c)   (i)   F   (2)
         (ii)   first violins ; solo cello ; first clarinet   (3)

   (d)   1   minor 10th / compound minor 3rd   (2)
         2   minor 6th   (2)

   (e)   (i)   false   (2)
         (ii)   true   (2)
         (iii)   true   (2)

Theory Paper   Grade 7   2014   B
Model Answers

1   *There are many ways of completing this question. The specimen completion below would receive full marks.*   (15)
The passage is adapted from J. S. Bach, Verse 3 from Cantata 'Lobe den Herren, den mächtigen König der Ehren',
BWV 137.

2 *There are many ways of completing this question. The specimen completion below would receive full marks.* (15)
The passage is adapted from Schubert, third movement of Sonata in B flat major, D. 960, bars 1–8 and 87–90.

3   *There are many ways of completing this question. Either of the specimen completions below would receive full marks.* (20)

EITHER

(a)   *The passage is adapted from Quilter, 'Music, when soft voices die', Op. 25 No. 5, beginning at bar 3.*

OR

(b)   *The given opening is printed in grey in order to distinguish it from the completion, but candidates must include the opening in their answer.*
bassoon

4   *The source of the extract is Clementi, second movement of Piano Sonata, Op. 34 No. 2, beginning at bar 85.*

(a)   Bar 5   diminished 7th   (3)
      Bar 18 V^7a / V^7a major   Key   E♭ major   (4)

(b)   *All possible answers are shown on the extract reproduced opposite. For full marks, candidates need to identify only one example of each answer.*

B	Bar	7 / 8	(2)
C	Bars	19–23	(2)
D	Bar	23	(2)
E	Bar	20 / 21	(2)

8

(c)   X   lower auxiliary note / chromatic lower auxiliary note   (2)

Y   appoggiatura / leaning note   (2)

(d) Similarity   melodic shape / harmony   (1)

One mark will be awarded (up to a maximum of three marks) for each correct reference to the following:
Differences ***fz*** and ***p*** markings in bars 11–12 / *con espress.* marking in bar 15 /   (3)
        articulation in right-hand part / syncopated rhythm in right-hand
        part of bars 15–16 / broken chord in right-hand part of bars 15–16 /
        first quaver in left-hand part of bar 15 / semiquaver rests in bars 15–16

(e)   true   (2)

5   *The source of the extract is Glazunov, first movement of Violin Concerto, Op. 82, beginning at bar 71.*

(a)   roll / drum roll / rapid reiteration of the same note   (2)
       divided / divided into two parts   (2)
       getting softer / dying away   (2)

(b)   (i)   second clarinet ;   (3)
             first violins ; first clarinet
       (ii)   double basses ; cellos ; first bassoon   (3)

(c)   (i)   Clarinets   (4)

(ii)   Horns   (3)

10

(d) *All possible answers are shown on the extract reproduced below. For B, candidates must identify one note in each section in the relevant bar to receive full marks.*

B   Bar   4 / 6

C   Bar   4

(2)

(2)

(e)   false

(2)

Theory Paper   Grade 7   2014   C
Model Answers

1   *There are many ways of completing this question. The specimen completion below would receive full marks.* (15)
The passage is adapted from Handel, fourth movement of Sonata in C minor, HWV 366.

etc.

2   *There are many ways of completing this question. The specimen completion below would receive full marks.* (15)
The passage is adapted from J. S. Bach, Chorale 'Gott der Vater wohn' uns bei', BWV 317 (Riemenschneider No. 135),
beginning in bar 8.

3   *There are many ways of completing this question. Either of the specimen completions below would receive full marks.* (20)

EITHER

(a)   *The passage is adapted from Stanford, Cuttin' Rushes, Op. 77 No. 3, beginning in bar 4.*

OR

(b)   *The answer uses the optional given opening, which is printed in grey in order to distinguish it from the completion.*

trombone

4   *The source of the extract is Mendelssohn, third movement of Violin Sonata, Op. 4.*

(a)   Bar 8   diminished 7th   (3)

Bar 12   ii°⁷a / II⁷a diminished / iv⁶d / IV⁶d minor   Key   F minor   (4)

(b)      (3)

(c)   Similarities   same melody   (1)

both played at same dynamic   (1)

One mark will be awarded (up to a maximum of two marks) for each correct reference to the following:

Differences   violin not playing in bars 1–4 *or* melody in violin in bars 11–14 /   (2)
harmony in bars 2 and 12 / articulation in the melody

(d)   *All possible answers are shown on the extract reproduced below. For full marks, candidates need to identify only one example of each answer.*

B   Bar   29   (2)

C   Bar   13   (2)

D   Bar   17 / 25   (2)

14

(e)　X　changing note (2)
　　　Y　appoggiatura / leaning note (2)

(f)　　　　　　　　　　　　　　　　　Mendelssohn (1)

5　*The source of the extract is Fauré, third movement of Pelléas et Mélisande, Op. 80, beginning at bar 77.*

(a)　(i)　harp (2)
　　(ii)　violas (2)
　　(iii)　2 (2)
　　(iv)　4 (2)
　　(v)　cor anglais (2)

(b)　much / very (1)
　　up-bow (2)
　　all players / no longer divided / unison (2)
　　harmonic / sounding an octave higher than written (2)

(c)　(i)　Horn (2)

(ii)　Clarinet (2)

(d)　1　major 9th / compound major 2nd (2)
　　2　minor 10th / compound minor 3rd (2)

15

Theory Paper   Grade 7   2014   S
Model Answers

1   *There are many ways of completing this question. The specimen completion below would receive full marks.*   (15)
    The passage is adapted from Telemann, first movement of Sonata in B minor, TWV 41:h3.

2   *There are many ways of completing this question. The specimen completion below would receive full marks.*   (15)
    The passage is adapted from J. S. Bach, Chorale 'Seelenbräutigam, Jesu, Gottes Lamm', BWV 409 (Riemenschneider No. 141), beginning at bar 4.

3   *There are many ways of completing this question. Either of the specimen completions below would receive full marks.* (20)

EITHER

(a)   *The passage is adapted from Verdi, 'Parmi veder le lagrime' from Act II of Rigoletto, beginning at bar 60.*

OR

(b)   *The given opening is printed in grey in order to distinguish it from the completion, but candidates must include the opening in their answer.*

oboe

4   *The source of the extract is Gade, Canzonette, Op. 19 No. 3.*

(a)   *One mark will be awarded (up to a maximum of two marks) for each correct reference to the following:*
   Similarities   melodic shape / rhythm of right-hand part / **rit.** / hairpin down to **p**   (2)

   One mark will be awarded (up to a maximum of three marks) for each correct reference to the following:
   Differences   pitch / **fz** in bar 18 / pedal marking in bar 7 / rhythm of left-hand part / articulation   (3)

(b)   Bar 6   Neapolitan 6th / ♭IIb / ♭IIb major   Key   A minor   (4)

        Bar 18   IV⁷a / IV⁷a major   Key   C major   (4)

(c)   *All possible answers are shown on the extract reproduced below.*

    B   Bar   7   (2)

    C   Bars   4–5   (2)

    D   Bar   17   (2)

    E   Bar   12   (2)

18

(d)   *One mark will be awarded (up to a maximum of three marks) for each correct reference to the following:*
staccato / **pp** marking / regular semiquaver movement in right-hand part /
scalic, repetitive pattern in right-hand part (3)

(e)   1800–1900   (1)

5   *The source of the extract is Bartók, second movement of Orchestral Suite No. 2, Op. 4, beginning four bars before rehearsal mark 31.*

(a)   playfully / jokingly / humorously   (2)
roll / drum roll / rapid reiteration of the same note   (2)
measured semiquavers / repeated semiquavers   (2)
both players   (2)

(b)   (i)   (4)

       (ii)   (3)

(c)   1   diminished 12th / compound diminished 5th   (2)
       2   major 13th / compound major 6th   (2)

(d)   (i)   true   (2)
       (ii)   true   (2)

(e)   Bartók   (1)

harmonic language / use of Italian terms makes Debussy unlikely   (1)

Music Theory Past Papers 2014 Model Answers

Model answers for four past papers from ABRSM's 2014 Theory exams for Grade 7

Key features:

- a list of correct answers where appropriate
- a selection of likely options where the answer can be expressed in a variety of ways
- a single exemplar where a composition-style answer is required

Support material for ABRSM Theory exams

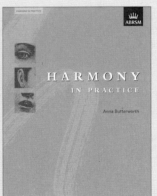

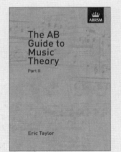

ABRSM
24 Portland Place
London W1B 1LU
United Kingdom

www.abrsm.org

ABRSM is the exam board of the Royal Schools of Music. We are committed to actively supporting high-quality music-making, learning and development throughout the world, and to producing the best possible resources for music teachers and students.

ISBN 978-1-84849-718-4